IF YOU GIVE A TEACHER A BOOK

Using Picture Books to Teach the Traits of Writing

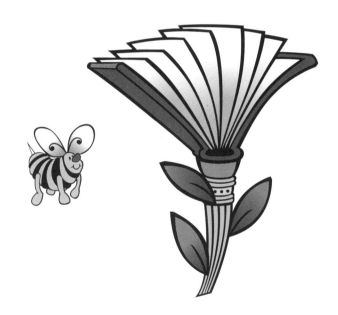

Karen A. Gibson & Sheila L. Wise

UpstartBooks

Janesville, Wisconsin

Acknowledgements
Thank you to the teachers of the Pasadena Independent School District
who are always willing to share.
Also, a huge thanks to the Curriculum and Instruction Department of the
Pasadena Independent School District who are more like family than co-workers!
—Karen and Sheila

For my husband, Rex who loves and supports me always!
For my girls, Joy and Amanda who listen enthusiastically when I find my
"new favorite children's book" to read to them.
For my parents who value education and have been my encouragement.
—Sheila

To Caleb, my first grandson. May you continue to find joy in books as I find joy in you.
—Karen

Published by UpstartBooks
401 S. Wright Rd.
Janesville, Wisconsin 53547
1-800-448-4887

© Karen A. Gibson and Sheila L. Wise, 2008
Cover design: Debra Neu

The paper used in this publication meets the minimum req .rements of American National
Standard for Information Science — Permanence of P? er for Printed Library Material.
ANSI/NISO Z39.48-1992.

Table of Contents

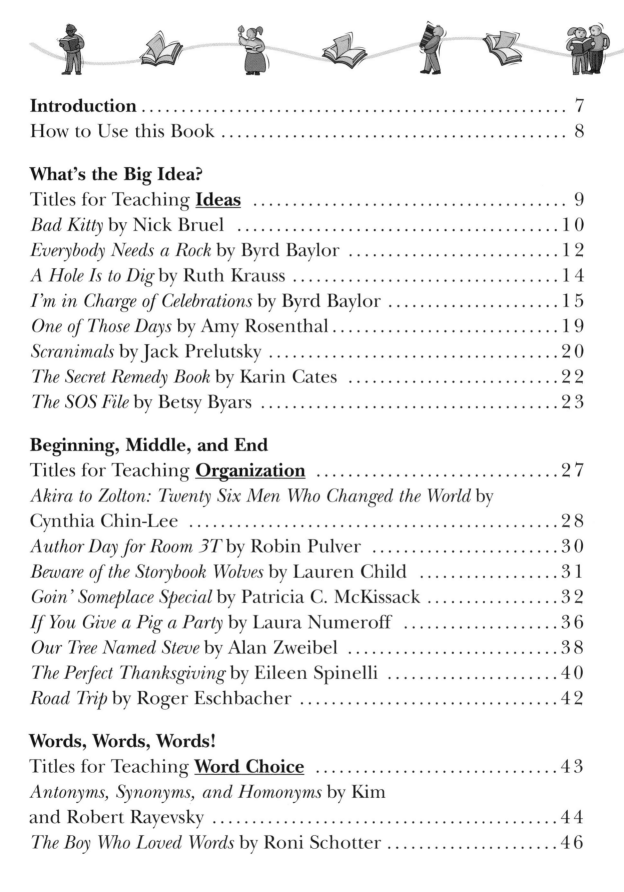

Introduction 7

How to Use this Book 8

What's the Big Idea?

Titles for Teaching **Ideas** 9

Bad Kitty by Nick Bruel 10

Everybody Needs a Rock by Byrd Baylor 12

A Hole Is to Dig by Ruth Krauss 14

I'm in Charge of Celebrations by Byrd Baylor 15

One of Those Days by Amy Rosenthal 19

Scranimals by Jack Prelutsky 20

The Secret Remedy Book by Karin Cates 22

The SOS File by Betsy Byars 23

Beginning, Middle, and End

Titles for Teaching **Organization** 27

Akira to Zolton: Twenty Six Men Who Changed the World by
Cynthia Chin-Lee 28

Author Day for Room 3T by Robin Pulver 30

Beware of the Storybook Wolves by Lauren Child 31

Goin' Someplace Special by Patricia C. McKissack .. 32

If You Give a Pig a Party by Laura Numeroff 36

Our Tree Named Steve by Alan Zweibel 38

The Perfect Thanksgiving by Eileen Spinelli 40

Road Trip by Roger Eschbacher 42

Words, Words, Words!

Titles for Teaching **Word Choice** 43

Antonyms, Synonyms, and Homonyms by Kim
and Robert Rayevsky 44

The Boy Who Loved Words by Roni Schotter 46

Duke Ellington by Andrea Davis Pinkney 50

Fancy Nancy by Jane O'Connor 52

Giving Thanks by Jonathan London 54

Max's Words by Kate Banks 55

Mom and Dad Are Palindromes by Mark Shulman 57

Mr. George Baker by Amy Hest 59

Got Rhythm?

Titles for Teaching **<u>Sentence Fluency</u>** 61

An Angel for Solomon Singer by Cynthia Rylant 62

Dick and Jane—A Christmas Story by Larry Ruppert 64

Hello, Harvest Moon by Ralph Fletcher 66

Heroes and She-roes Poems of Amazing and Everyday Heroes
by J. Patrick Lewis 68

Library Lil by Suzanne Williams 70

Night Noises by Mem Fox 74

The Wheels on the School Bus by Mary-Alice Moore 76

Wonderful Words: Poems about Reading, Writing, Speaking, and Listening
by Lee Bennett Hopkins 79

Let's Get Personal!

Titles for Teaching **<u>Voice</u>** 81

Dear Mrs. LaRue—Letters from Obedience School
by Mark Teague 82

Diary of a Worm by Doreen Cronin 83

I Wanna Iguana by Karen Kaufman Orloff 84

The Mysteries of Harris Burdick by Chris Van Allsburg 85

Rosy Cole's Memoir Explosion by Sheila Greenwald 86

The True Story of the Three Little Pigs by Jon Scieszka 88

Voices in the Park by Anthony Browne 89

Who is Melvin Bubble? by Nick Bruel 91

Capitals, Periods, and Commas—Oh, My!

Titles for Teaching **<u>Conventions</u>** 93

Alfie the Apostrophe by Rose Maria Donohue 94

*Brain Juice English, Fresh Squeezed! 40 Thirst-for-knowledge-
quenching-poems* by Carol Diggory Shields 97

Eats, Shoots & Leaves by Lynne Truss 98

The Hello, Goodbye Window by Norton Juster 99

The Important Book by Margaret Wise Brown 102

Nouns and Verbs Have a Field Day by Robin Pulver 105

Punctuation Takes a Vacation by Robin Pulver 107

The Stinky Cheese Man and Other Fairly Stupid Tales
by Jon Scieszka 108

It's All About the Looks!
Titles for Teaching **Presentation** 111

The Adventures of the Dish and the Spoon by Mini Grey 112

Can You See What I See? Once Upon a Time by Walter Wick 114

Come to My Party and Other Shape Poems by Heidi Roemer 116

Fairytale News by Colin and Jacqui Hawkins 118

I Spy Christmas: A Book of Christmas Riddles by Jean Marzollo . 119

The Jolly Postman and Other People's Letters
by Janet and Alan Ahlberg 120

Look at My Book: How Kids Can Write and Illustrate Terrific Books
by Loreen Leedy 121

The Popcorn Book by Tomie de Paola 122

Index by Author 123

Index by Title 124

Introduction

We have worked with teachers in a large metropolitan school district who teach students in grades three through twelve, and we have heard over and over again that writing is the most difficult subject to teach. Writing is often the area where teachers feel most insecure as educators. For some teachers, writing comes naturally, thus making it difficult to explain the writing process to students. Other teachers feel insecure in their own writing skills, which makes the writing instruction often painful.

In researching ways to help teachers with writing instruction, we have found that the use of picture books to demonstrate excellent writing is a tremendous tool. As Laminack and Wadsworth assert in their excellent book, *Learning Under the Influence of Language and Literature: Making the Most of Read-Alouds Across the Day,* "As teachers, we must trust our students as learners and enlist writers as our co-teachers. Writers of children's books typically know their audience well and approach their craft with that audience in mind" (Heinemann, 2006).

In *If You Give a Teacher a Book,* we have enlisted many authors of picture books as your co-teachers. As your students experience the writing of published authors, and as you guide them through the experience with the strategies contained in the following pages, you will be amazed that the instruction of writing can actually be enjoyable!

Karen and Sheila

How to Use this Book

If You Give a Teacher a Book provides you with strategies and lessons to make using picture books for writing instruction both pleasant and educational for your students. The lessons are designed in such a way that the media specialist and teacher can collaborate. The book can be read first in the library for enjoyment, followed by a time of focused discussion on the author's craft of writing. The classroom teacher can then follow up by rereading the book in order to present the writing activity.

Many teachers organize their writing instruction around the following traits of writing—Ideas, Organization, Word Choice, Sentence Fluency, Voice, Conventions, and Presentation. Therefore, each lesson in *If You Give a Teacher a Book* includes a summary of the story, a writing prompt, a lesson that reinforces the skill, and a list of the writing traits which are highlighted in the lesson. The lessons can sometimes be used for multiple traits, so we have listed the primary trait first.

Happy reading and writing!

What's the Big Idea?

Titles for Teaching Ideas

In the Traits of Writing, "**Ideas**" means the overall message of the piece of writing is presented with clarity, focus, and detail.

Evidence of Good Ideas

- The topic is narrowed and has relevant details.
- The topic is fresh and original.
- The details about the topic "show" the reader rather than just "tell."

Books Used in this Chapter

Bad Kitty by Nick Bruel. Roaring Brook Press, 2005.

Everybody Needs a Rock by Byrd Baylor. Aladdin, 1974.

A Hole is to Dig by Ruth Krauss. HarperCollins, 1952.

I'm In Charge of Celebrations by Byrd Baylor. Simon & Schuster, 1986.

One of Those Days by Amy Rosenthal. Putnam, 2006.

Scranimals by Jack Prelutsky. Scholastic, 2002.

The Secret Remedy Book by Karin Cates. Scholastic, 2003.

The SOS File by Betsy Byars. Henry Holt & Company, 2004.

Bad Kitty

by Nick Bruel

Summary

In this unique alphabet book, a kitty decides to be very bad when she discovers there is no food in the house.

Prompt

Write about a time when you got in trouble for being bad.

Lesson

1. Read *Bad Kitty* aloud to the class.

2. Point out to the students how the story ends with the kitty learning that she will have to share her food with the new puppy.

3. Put one set of die-cut letters in each of two containers. Have students choose one letter for Part 1 of the class book and one letter for Part 2 of the class book. (If you have less than 26 students in your class, some students will have two letters. If you have more than 26 students in your class, allow some students to work together.)

4. Follow the pattern on page 11 to create the class book.

Traits Addressed

Ideas, Organization, and
Presentation

Format for Class Book

Front Cover:

Ask one of the students to create a cover showing a kitty and a puppy. Students can create a new title for the book, or it can be titled "Bad Kitty Part Two."

Page 1:

Text: When Kitty discovered that she was going to have to share her food with the family's new puppy, she decided that the puppy would have to eat … (Choose a student to illustrate this page.)

Pages 2–27:

Using the first letter of the alphabet that each student chose, they will illustrate and label an unpopular food that begins with their letter on individual pages.

Page 28:

Text: Puppy was not happy, not happy at all. That's when he decided he would be extra nice to Kitty. He … (Choose a student to illustrate this page.)

Pages 29–54:

Using the second letter of the alphabet that each student chose, they will illustrate and write about a kind thing Puppy will do for Kitty to make her like him using their alphabet letter. Each letter will be on an individual page.

Page 55:

Text: Because Puppy was so kind to Kitty, she decided they could be best friends. They lived and played together happily ever after. Your students might want to make up an alternate ending. (Choose a student to illustrate this page.)

Back Cover:

Have each student author sign his/her name, filling the back cover with signatures.

Bind the book together for all to enjoy.

Everybody Needs a Rock

by Byrd Baylor; illustrated by Peter Parnall

Summary

The narrator of this book believes that each and every person needs a rock to call his or her own. Each person's rock will be unique and special, but it is important to use the 10 rules in the book to find the perfect rock.

Prompt

Write a composition entitled "Everybody Needs a _____."

(Each student can choose something that they think everyone needs.)

Lesson

1. Read the first three pages of text of *Everybody Needs a Rock* aloud to the students.

2. Lead the students to notice how the author interjects her voice into the book with quotes such as, "I'm sorry for the kids who don't have a rock for a friend."

3. Continue reading the author's 10 rules for finding a rock.

4. Discuss how the author puts the rules into poetic format.

5. Encourage the students to notice how the author elaborates each rule so that the reader has a mental picture of finding a rock.

6. Have students fill in the Prewriting form (page 13) before they write their composition, "Everybody Needs a _____."

Traits Addressed

Ideas, Organization, Voice, and Conventions

Prewriting

Choose something that you think everyone needs.

"Everybody Needs a _____ "

Now create your own 10 rules for finding a _____.

Rules:

1. _____
2. _____
3. _____
4. _____
5. _____
6. _____
7. _____
8. _____
9. _____
10. _____

Now that you have determined what you think everyone needs and have your 10 basic rules for getting it, write a composition in which you elaborate on these rules so that you can convince your readers.

A Hole Is to Dig

by Ruth Krauss; illustrated by Maurice Sendak

Summary

The subtitle of *A Hole Is to Dig* is "A First Book of First Definitions." The book is filled with creative and thought-provoking definitions such as "a lap is so you don't get crumbs on the floor" and "rugs are so dogs have napkins."

Prompt

Write and illustrate your own book of creative definitions.

Lesson

1. Read *A Hole Is to Dig* aloud to students.

2. Have students choose their favorite definitions and explain why they like them and how they are different from the dictionary definition.

3. Have students look around the classroom and call out names of objects that will be added to a class list.

4. Have each student choose one of the objects on the list and write a creative definition.

5. Have each child illustrate his or her definition.

6. Compile the definitions into a class book.

Traits Addressed

Ideas and Word Choice

I'm in Charge of Celebrations

by Byrd Baylor

Summary

Byrd Baylor shares celebrations of nature in the desert in this beautifully written book. These are not your typical celebrations, but rather things like "The Time of Falling Stars" in the middle of August and "Rainbow Celebration Day."

Prompt

Write about something you would like to celebrate.

Lesson

1. Read *I'm in Charge of Celebrations* aloud to the students.

2. On the board, list some of the things celebrated in the book and the rules for what it takes to be a celebration:

   Dust Devil Day
   Rainbow Celebration Day
   Green Cloud Day
   Coyote Day

3. To get them thinking, have students fill in the "I'm in Charge of Celebrations" chart (page 17) with things they already celebrate, things they use to celebrate, and celebration words.

> "It has to be something I plan to remember the rest of my life. You can tell what's worth a celebration because your heart will POUND and you'll feel like you're standing on top of a mountain and you'll catch your breath like you were breathing some new kind of air."
>
> —from *I'm in Charge of Celebrations*

4. Have students brainstorm ideas for a celebration they would like to have.

5. Using their ideas and the chart, have the students write about something they would like to celebrate. There's a reproducible sheet on page 18 for students to use for their compositions.

6. They can decorate the paper for their final copy and make a celebration presentation to the class.

Traits Addressed

Ideas, Word Choice, Sentence Fluency, and Organization

I'm in Charge of Celebrations!

Types of Celebrations	Things Used to Celebrate	Celebration Words

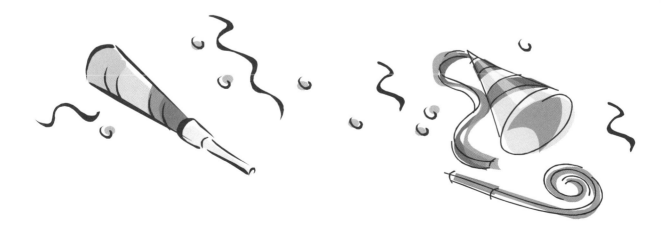

I'm in Charge of Celebrations!

Date: _____

Celebration: _____

_____

_____

_____

_____

_____

_____

_____

_____

_____

_____

_____

_____

One of Those Days

by Amy Krouse Rosenthal and Rebecca Daughty

Summary

Some days just don't turn out the way you had planned and the authors refer to these days a "one of those days." Thankfully, there is always tomorrow to look forward to.

Prompt

Write about a day when things did not go as you had planned.

Lesson

1. Ask students if they have ever had a bad day. Volunteers can list some of the reasons they had a bad day.

2. Read *One of Those Days* aloud to the class.

3. After reading and discussing the book, read aloud the popular *Alexander and the Terrible, Horrible, No Good, Very Bad Day* by Judith Viorst.

4. Brainstorm a class list of the many "one of those days" that Alexander is having. Example: Had to eat lima beans day.

5. Start a class list of bad days.

6. After keeping the list long enough to have a good selection, have students choose one of the bad days and write a composition about it.

7. Encourage students to have a beginning, middle, and end to their story.

8. You might follow the same pattern and write another composition about students' good days rather than bad days.

Traits Addressed

Ideas, Organization, and Voice

Scranimals

by Jack Prelutsky

Summary

This delightful book of poems sparks the imagination. Jack Prelutsky has teamed up with illustrator Peter Sís to bring the reader a variety of mixed-up animal poems such as "Avocadodos," "Bananaconda," and "Radishark" by combining the characteristics of food and animals.

Prompt

Write a story or poem about a unique, mixed-up animal.

Lesson

1. Read "The Journey" from *Scranimals*.

2. List some of the different scranimals from the book on the board. Let the students brainstorm some other scranimals.

   Spinachickens
   Potatoad
   Porcupinapple

3. Using the Scranimals Brainstorming Chart on page 21, have students begin to combine things from each category until they come up with one they want to write a poem or composition about.

4. Students can draw their scranimal and make a presentation to the class introducing him/her.

Traits Addressed

Ideas, Organization, Sentence Fluency, Word Choice, and Presentation

Scranimals Brainstorming Chart

	Animals	Birds	Fish	Insects	Plants	Vegetables	Fruit

The Secret Remedy Book

by Karin Cates; illustrated by Wendy Anderson Halperin

Summary

Lolly has always wished to visit her Auntie Zep all by herself, but when she finally gets the chance to stay with her for a month without her parents, Lolly finds that she is very lonesome. Auntie Zep suggests that they find the Secret Remedy book in the old trunk and the adventure begins.

Prompt

Write your own Secret Remedies for when you are feeling lonesome.

Lesson

1. Read *The Secret Remedy Book* to students.

2. Discuss the way the author organized the book. First she introduced the characters and the conflict—Lolly was homesick for her parents. Then the author explained the idea of the secret remedies for loneliness. Next came the explanation of the seven remedies. Finally, the author provided the conclusion of the story.

3. Have the students brainstorm remedies they might use for homesickness, sadness, or loneliness. Write their responses on the board.

4. Return to the book and notice how the author listed each remedy and then elaborated on how Lolly used that remedy to help her feel better.

5. Ask each student to pick seven remedies of their own and elaborate on the remedies as the author did.

Traits Addressed

Ideas, Organization, Voice, and Sentence Fluency

The SOS File

by Betsy Byars, Betsy Duffey, and Laurie Myers

Summary

For fun and extra credit, Mr. Magro's students have written about their biggest emergencies. The papers were collected into an SOS File. At the end of the year Mr. Magro announces that everyone who wrote a story got extra credit except for one. He proceeds to read the stories one by one as the students listen anxiously to find out who didn't get the extra credit. Each story is a gem that will tickle your funny bone and bring you to tears.

Prompt

Write about a time when you were involved in an emergency.

Lesson

1. Discuss the meaning of "SOS." A good explanation can be found at www.boatsafe.com/nauticalknowhow/060199tip6.htm.

2. Read the introduction of *The SOS File*—"The Day Arrives" to the students.

3. Discuss different kinds of emergencies.

4. Read several of the stories from *The SOS File* aloud, and stop to point out different traits you want to highlight.

    a. Example: Organization—Openings: "A Bear Tale"—"One day last June, Abraham Lincoln saved my life."

    b. Example: Voice: "The Chocolate SOS."

5. Have the students write their own SOS story using the graphic organizer on page 25 as a guide. When they're finished have them look

over their story for one object or word that best symbolizes the main idea/theme of their story. You may want to show some picture examples from the book.

Traits Addressed

Ideas, Organization, and Voice

My SOS

Title:_____

What was the event?

Who was involved?

Was there any talking/dialogue?

What was going on in your mind?

What objects or actions do you remember?

What did you hear, smell, touch, or taste?

What object best symbolizes this event? Draw it here.

Describe all the feelings you had during this event.

Beginning, Middle, and End

Titles for Teaching Organization

In the Traits of Writing, **"Organization"** is how a piece of writing is put together using a clear and logical pattern.

Evidence of Good Organization

- The piece has a good sense of sequence.

- The piece has a powerful lead, strong transitions, and a solid conclusion.

- The piece has an internal structure that connects ideas and develops anticipation in the reader.

Books Used in this Chapter

Akira to Zolton: Twenty Six Men Who Changed the World by Cynthia Chin-Lee. Charlesbridge, 2006.

Author Day for Room 3T by Robin Pulver. Clarion Books, 2005.

Beware of the Storybook Wolves by Lauren Child. Hodder and Stoughton, 2000.

Goin' Someplace Special by Patricia C. McKissack. Atheneum Books for Young Reaers, 2006.

If You Give a Pig a Party by Laura Numeroff. Laura Geringer Books, 2005.

Our Tree Named Steve by Alan Zweibel. Putnam, 2005.

The Perfect Thanksgiving by Eileen Spinelli. Henry Holt & Company, 2003.

Road Trip by Roger Eschbacher. Dial. 2006.

Akira to Zoltan
Twenty-Six Men Who Changed the World

by Cynthia Chin-Lee; illustrated by Megan Halsey and Sean Addy

Summary

This alphabet book highlights twenty-six little-known men, one for each letter of the alphabet, whose accomplishments made the world a better place.

Prompt

Write about a person you know or whom you have studied who has done something to make the world a better place.

Lesson

1. *Akira to Zoltan: Twenty-Six Men Who Changed the World* should be read aloud over several weeks, highlighting one or two people per day.

2. Discuss how the author organized the book alphabetically by choosing one influential person for each letter of the alphabet.

3. Discuss the research that had to be conducted to write each person's short biographical sketch.

4. Explain that a class project will be to write a class alphabet book about twenty-six people who have changed our school.

5. Each class member can choose one person, adult or student, who has had a positive impact on the school. Keep track of the people chosen, matching them to letters of the alphabet. First or last names may be used.

6. Each student writes a short biographical sketch of the person they have chosen.

7. Compile the biographies into alphabetical order. (It is okay if all the letters are not used, since it is more important to highlight important people than to use each letter.)

8. Have a class author party and invite the people highlighted in the book to attend. Have each author read his/her own work.

Traits Addressed

Organization, Ideas, and Presentation

Author Day for Room 3T

by Robin Pulver; illustrated by Chuck Richards

Summary

A third grade class is excited about a visit from their favorite author, Harry Bookman. When the author arrives, they get an unexpected surprise. The book ends with "Harry Bookman's Tips for Hosting a Successful Author Visit."

Prompts

Write about a time when things did not turn out as you expected.

Write directions for making or doing something.

Lesson

1. Read *Author Day for Room 3T* aloud to the students. Stop at the end of the story before you get to "Harry Bookman's Tips for Hosting a Successful Author Visit."

2. Discuss how the chimpanzee was able to trick the students and teachers into believing that he was the visiting author.

3. Read "Harry Bookman's Tips for Hosting a Successful Author Visit" which is at the end of the book.

4. Explain that this page is a special type of writing called "technical writing."

5. Discuss the different formats of technical writing such as sequential steps and bulleted ideas.

6. Have students write a piece of technical writing explaining how to make or do something.

Traits Addressed

Organization and Conventions

Beware of the Storybook Wolves

by Lauren Child

Summary

Herb is frightened of the Big Bad Wolf in his bedtime storybook. One night his mother forgets to take the storybook with her when she leaves the room. The big bad wolf escapes from the book and Herb must figure out a way to keep from being eaten.

Prompt

Write about a fairy tale character who escapes from a book and joins you at school for the day.

Lesson

1. Read *Beware of the Storybook Wolves* aloud to the students.

2. Discuss the organization of a fairy tale. Remind students that most fairy tales begin with a common phrase such as "once upon a time." In the middle of the story, the author develops a challenge for the main character to overcome. Most fairy tales end happily with the phrase, "and they lived happily ever after."

3. Have students brainstorm a list of fairy tale characters. Write the names of the characters on the board.

4. Discuss how some of the characters would react to situations in the classroom because of the distinctive character traits they possess. Example: If the Big Bad Wolf were given a test, he would probably huff and puff and blow the teacher down. On the other hand, if the third little pig were given a test, he would work diligently to make a good grade.

5. Have students write a composition using one or more of the fairy tale characters out of their original story setting. They should be sure that the character retains traits from the original story.

Traits Addressed

Organization, Ideas, and Voice

Goin' Someplace Special

by Patricia C. McKissack; illustrated by Jerry Pinkney

Summary

'Tricia Ann is finally old enough to go "Someplace Special" by herself. She gets all dressed up and heads off to her favorite spot in the world, recounting the events that happen along the way.

Prompts

Write about "Someplace Special" you have been.

Write about your favorite spot in the world.

Lesson

1. Read Goin' Someplace Special aloud to students.

2. As students listen, have them list examples on the "Goin' Someplace Special" chart (page 33) of what 'Tricia Ann sees, hears, and feels as she travels to her favorite spot in the world.

3. Discuss both positive and negative words they have written down.

4. Let students brainstorm ideas for their own "Someplace Special."

5. Have students fill in the "My Someplace Special" chart (page 34) as they write about their trip to someplace special.

6. Have students use the "Goin' to My Favorite Spot in the World" map (page 35) to draw a route to their favorite spot.

Traits Addressed

Organization, Ideas, and Word Choice

Goin' Someplace Special

Using the book, *Goin' Someplace Special,* fill in the chart with things 'Tricia saw, heard, and felt as she made her way to the public library.

What 'Tricia SAW	What 'Tricia HEARD	What 'Tricia FELT

My Someplace Special

Thinking about your trip to Someplace Special, write what you saw, heard, and felt along the way.

What I SAW	What I HEARD	What I FELT

Goin' to my Favorite Spot in the World

Start Here

Someplace Special

If You Give a Pig a Party

By Laura Numeroff

Summary

Pig from *If You Give a Pig a Pancake* is up to her old ways, only this time it is a party she's after. She wants balloons, her favorite dress, and all her friends to be involved. Laura Numeroff's cause-and-effect style make this book appealing to children.

Prompts

Write about a fun party you attended or would like to have.

Write directions for how to plan a party.

Write a story using the same cause-and-effect structure that Laura Numeroff uses in *If You Give a Pig a Party*.

Lesson

1. Read *If You Give a Pig a Party* to students.
2. Have them think about a party they have attended and let them brainstorm funny or unusual events. Next have them circle one event to write about.
3. Students should concentrate on organization by having a catchy beginning, lots of voice in the middle, and a great ending.
4. Give students the Party Hat pattern (page 37). Let them decorate the front using one thing that symbolizes something in their composition.
5. Have them share their stories while wearing their hats.

Traits Addressed

Organization, Voice, and Presentation

Party Hat

cut slits

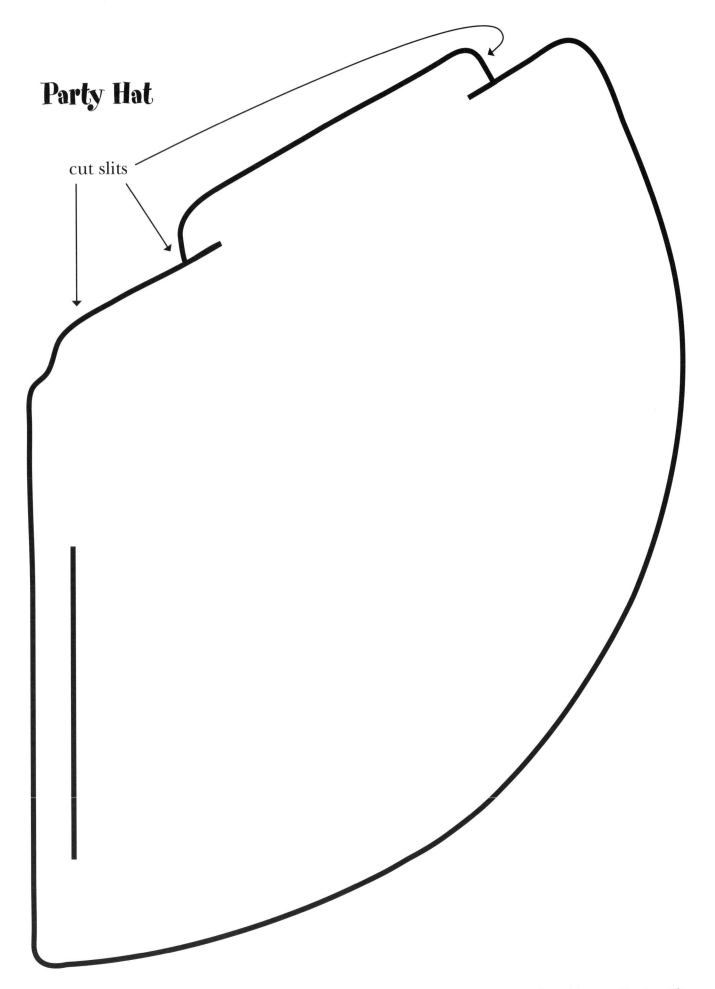

Our Tree Named Steve

by Alan Zweibel; illustrated by David Catrow

Summary

A father writes a letter to his children recounting the role that a special tree, whom the family named Steve, has played in their lives.

Prompt

Write a letter explaining how a special person or object has made an impact on your life.

Lesson

1. Read *Our Tree Named Steve* aloud to the students.

2. Explain that the letter the father wrote to his children became a narrative of the tree's important role in the family's life.

3. Discuss how the father followed a sequential timeline when writing the letter.

4. Using the Our Tree Named Steve Timeline on page 39, list the major events in the life of Steve the tree and the family who loved him.

5. Discuss the importance of organization when writing a narrative.

6. Encourage students to make a timeline of events before writing their letter.

Trait Addressed

Organization

Event 1	Event 2	Event 3	Event 4	Event 5	Event 6	Event 7	Event 8	Event 9	Event 10

Our Tree Named Steve Timeline

The Perfect Thanksgiving

by Eileen Spinelli

Summary

This is a story of how two families celebrate Thanksgiving. Family One seems to do everything perfectly while Family Two has disaster after disaster. In the end, however, the two families find they have one thing in common—how loving they are.

Prompt

Write about a typical Thanksgiving Day at your house.

Lesson

1. Read aloud *The Perfect Thanksgiving*.

2. Using the T-chart for Family One and Family Two on page 41, have students write the things that are opposite between the two families.

3. Have students list the things that typically go on at their own house on Thanksgiving Day. (Think about things like what foods are served, time of day they eat the meal, who is invited, what dress is appropriate, etc.)

4. Pair students up and have them compare and contrast the items on their lists.

5. Have students write a compare and contrast paper together using the information from both lists.

6. In Reader's Theater style, have the students read their papers to the class. Classmates could make a T-chart and fill in the opposite information as they listen. If the information is the same they could write that information below the T-chart.

Traits Addressed

Organization, Voice, and Word Choice

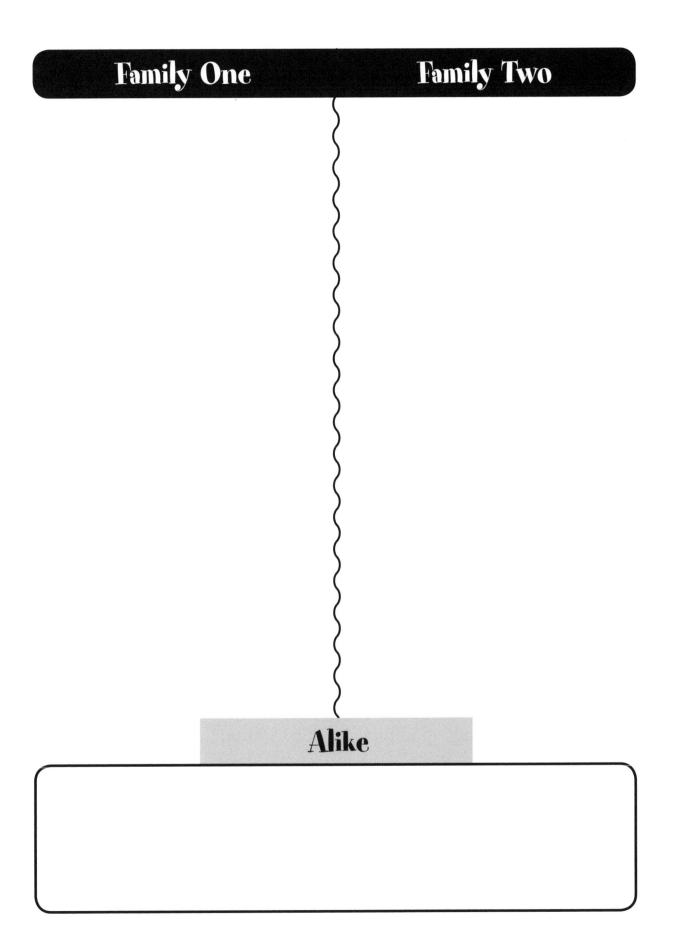

Family One   Family Two

Alike

Road Trip

by Roger Eschbacher; illustrated by Thor Wickstrom

Summary

A family embarks on a road trip across the country for a family reunion and experiences many exciting events along the way.

Prompt

Write about a trip you have taken or would like to take.

Lesson

1. Read *Road Trip* aloud to your students.

2. Discuss how the author wrote a poem about each event that took place on the journey in the order that they took place.

3. List the different events (titles of poems) on the board.

4. Explain to students that they are going to keep track of all the events that make up a normal school day. Examples: Pledge of Allegiance, morning announcements, math class, lunchtime, P.E., etc.

5. After compiling the list, let students pick one activity to write a poem about.

6. Compile the poems into a class book entitled "School Day."

Traits Addressed

Organization, Ideas, Voice, and Presentation

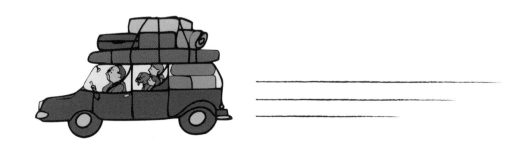

Words, Words, Words

Titles for Teaching Word Choice

In the Traits of Writing, **"Word Choice"** is all about catching the reader's attention using precise language that paints a clear picture.

Evidence of Good Word Choice

- Words clarify and expand the meaning.
- Words help the reader envision what is going on.
- Words are vivid, descriptive, and precise.

Books Used in this Chapter

Antonyms, Synonyms, and Homonyms by Kim and Robert Rayevsky. Holiday House, 2006.

The Boy Who Loved Words by Roni Schotter. Schwarz and Wade Books, 2006.

Duke Ellington by Andrea Davis Pinkney. Hyperion, 1998.

Fancy Nancy by Jane O'Connor. HarperCollins, 2005.

Giving Thanks by Jonathan London. Candlewick Press, 2003.

Max's Words by Kate Banks. Farrar, Straus and Giroux, 2006.

Mom and Dad Are Palindromes by Mark Shulman. Chronicle Books, 2006.

Mr. George Baker by Amy Hest. Candlewick Press, 2004.

Antonyms, Synonyms, and Homonyms

by Kim and Robert Rayevsky

Summary

A UFO lands in a city, and the alien aboard learns of antonyms, synonyms, and homonyms. The illustrations and the language study make this book unforgettable.

Prompt

Write about something unusual that has happened to you.

Lesson

1. Share the book *Antonyms, Synonyms, and Homonyms* with students.

2. Put the students in three groups. Give each group one of the Category Cards on page 45. Assign each group the task of thinking of as many words as possible that fit into their category.

3. Have each group choose the top 10 examples and make a poster with pictures either cut from magazines or hand drawn. Each poster should have the category and definition somewhere on the poster.

4. Place the posters on the wall to help remind students that as they write they need to make the best choice of words.

5. As an extension, you could let students add words as they see them in pieces they are reading.

Traits Addressed

Word Choice and Presentation

Category Cards

Antonyms are words with opposite meanings.

Example: hot/cold

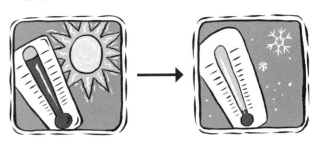

Synonyms are words that have the same meaning.

Example: scared/afraid

Homonyms are words that have the same sound and sometimes the same spelling, but different meanings.

Example: blue/blew & read/read

The Boy Who Loved Words

by Roni Schotter

Summary

While everyone else collects shells and teaspoons, Selig decides he wants to collect words. When he finds a word he likes, he writes it down on a piece of paper and puts it in his pocket. All the kids at school called Selig an oddball. In a dream a genie tells Selig he has a passion, but now he needs a purpose. So, Selig hits the road to find his purpose and along the way he also finds love.

Prompt

Write about something you collect or would like to collect.

Lesson

1. Ask students if anyone has a favorite word. Write the words on the board and ask why he/she likes the word. For example, I like the word "pi" because it is cute, but I like "superfluous" because of the way it sounds and how you have to move your mouth to say it.

2. Read *The Boy Who Loved Words* to students. Ask them to listen for words they like and list them as you read the story.

3. In the story, Selig puts his words on the branches of a tree, so have either a live tree or a paper one on which students can display their favorite words. You could also make a paper vocabulary quilt by placing different colored word squares together on a wall. See the examples on pages 47–48.

4. If students find one of their favorite words while reading, have them write down the sentence on the cards on page 49 to receive extra credit. If students use some of the words in their writing, they can also earn extra credit.

Traits Addressed

Word Choice and Ideas

Tree of Favorite Words

Quilt of Favorite Words

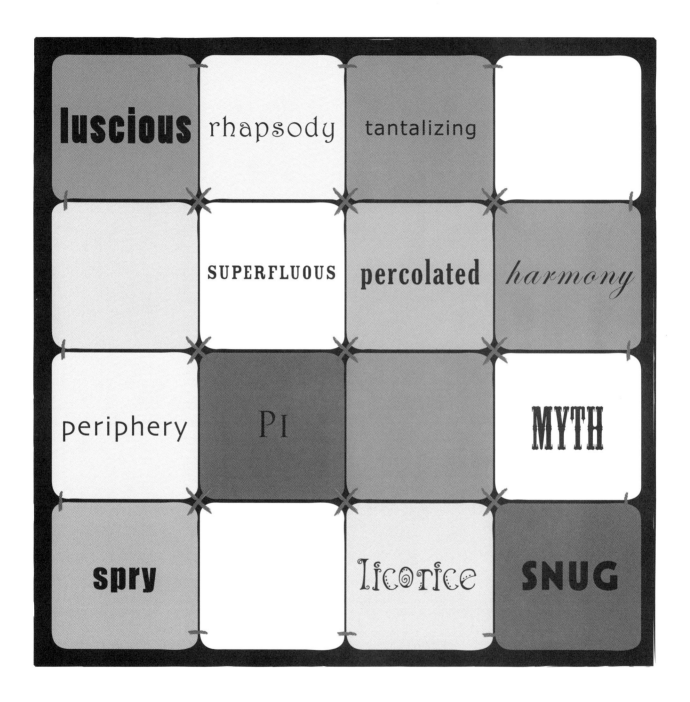

Favorite Word

Word _____ Date _____

Where Found _____

Sentence _____

Favorite Word

Word _____ Date _____

Where Found _____

Sentence _____

Favorite Word

Word _____ Date _____

Where Found _____

Sentence _____

Favorite Word

Word _____ Date _____

Where Found _____

Sentence _____

Duke Ellington

by Andrea Davis Pinkney

Summary

This lively story is a celebration of the life and music of Edward Kennedy "Duke" Ellington.

Prompt

Write about what success means to you.

Lesson

1. Ask the class to listen for phrases they like and make a list as you read *Duke Ellington* aloud.

2. Make a list of the favorite phrases and discuss why they like the phrases they chose.

3. Categorize some of the phrases. See the "Favorite Phrases from Duke Ellington" chart on page 51 for some examples. Discuss how figurative language and word choice help to make writing more interesting.

4. Discuss how color helps to bring the words to life in this book. Obtain some paint sample strips from your local hardware store. In groups have the students choose which color each phrase should be and be able to explain why. They must choose a specific shade and not just red.

5. Have the students go through a piece of their writing and see if they can add some "color" through the use of figurative language. Play some of Duke Ellington's music as the students work.

Traits Addressed

Word Choice, Voice, and Sentence Fluency

Favorite Phrases from Duke Ellington

Simile	Personification	Idioms
"curling his notes like a kite tail in the wind"	"the joint started to jump"	"cuttin' the rug"

Fancy Nancy

by Jane O'Connor; illustrated by Robin Preiss Glasser

Summary

Nancy is a young girl who always wants to be fancy rather than plain. Her favorite color is fuchsia, which is a fancy way of saying purple. Nancy convinces her plain family to be fancy with her for one night with some interesting results.

Prompt

Write about a subject of your own choice. When you have completed the composition, revise it by replacing at least 10 of the plain words with fancy words.

Lesson

1. Tell the students to listen for fancy words as you read *Fancy Nancy* aloud to them.

2. Using Part I of the chart on page 53. Be sure to notice the words in the illustrations.

3. After finishing the book, fill in Part II of the chart with the student's plain and fancy word lists.

4. Explain to students that there are times when fancy words are best, but that too many fancy words in a composition will make it sound foolish.

Trait Addressed

Word Choice

Plain & Fancy Words

Part I: List plain and fancy words from *Fancy Nancy*.

Plain Words	Fancy Words
Plain Example: purple	Fancy Example: fuchsia

Part II: Make a list of the class's plain and fancy words.

Plain Words	Fancy Words

Giving Thanks

by Jonathan London

Summary

A young boy and his father take a walk and admire things in nature they are thankful for.

Prompt

Write about something in nature you are thankful for.

Lesson

1. Read *Giving Thanks* aloud to students.

2. Discuss vivid verbs and descriptive words. Go back through the book and make a list of good, vivid, and descriptive words.

3. Re-read the following:

   Things of nature are a gift.

   In return, we must give something back.

   We must give thanks.

4. Have students take a nature walk and write down the gifts of nature they are thankful for.

5. Next have them write a composition about three of them.

6. Then have them go back through the paper, looking for words that need to be changed to be more vivid or descriptive. Circle the words that need to be changed and brainstorm better options.

7. Finally, have them rewrite using more descriptive words.

Traits Addressed

Word Choice and Sentence Fluency

Max's Words

by Kate Banks; illustrated by Boris Kulikov

Summary

Max's brothers collect coins and stamps and refuse to share, so Max decides to collect words. He learns that words make sentences and sentences make stories.

Prompt

Write about a subject of your choice. Include some of your favorite words in your composition.

Lesson

1. Read the book *Max's Words* aloud to the class.

2. Point out that Max puts his favorite words in categories.

3. Make a copy of the "My Favorite Words"chart on page 56 for each student.

4. Take the class to the library and allow them to browse through books to make their own list of favorite words. In addition to the categories that Max chose, students can put words in two additional categories of their choice.

5. Have students share their words with other students in cooperative groups. Group members can add other students' words to their own charts.

6. Students should keep their list of favorite words in a writing notebook to refer to when they need help choosing specific words for their writing.

Traits Addressed

Word Choice, Ideas, and Sentence Fluency

My Favorite Words

Small Words	Bigger Words	Words that Make Me Feel Good	Words of Things I Like to Eat	Favorite Color Words	_____ Words	_____ Words

Mom and Dad are Palindromes

by Mark Shulman and Adam McCauley

Summary

Bob's teacher, Miss Sim, taught the class about palindromes, words, and phrases that are spelled the same both forward and backward. Once he knows the meaning of the word, he cannot escape palindromes—they are everywhere.

Prompt

Write a composition using as many palindromes as possible.

Lesson

1. Read the book *Mom and Dad Are Palindromes* aloud to the class, showing the students some of the palindromes in the book.

2. Divide the class into groups of about five students.

3. Place the book *Mom and Dad Are Palindromes* in the writing center.

4. Number the pages of the book and assign each group of five students an equal number of pages.

5. Each group should find as many palindromes as possible on their assigned pages and write them on the class chart paper. Remind students to look carefully at both the text and illustrations. There are more than 101 palindromes in the book, even on the dedication page.

6. When the chart is full of palindromes from the book, brainstorm other palindromes and add to the list.

7. Have students write a composition (either individually or in groups) using as many palindromes as possible. Emphasize that the story should be fluent and interesting, not just a list of palindromes.

8. When students write the final draft of the composition, they should write the palindromes in a different-colored ink or (if done on a computer) in a different font to make them stand out.

Traits Addressed

Word Choice, Sentence Fluency, and Presentation

Mr. George Baker

by Amy Hest; illustrated by Jon J. Muth

Summary

Harry's friend, Mr. George Baker, is 100 years old. Some say he was once a famous drummer, and he can still dance and play the drums, but he has a problem that must be corrected. He cannot read.

Prompt

Write about something you would like to learn to do.

Lesson

1. Explain to the students that the author of this book uses repetition to add emphasis and to make her writing more interesting.

2. Ask students to listen for repeated words and phrases as you read *Mr. George Baker.*

3. Allow students to list the repeated phrases on a transparency made from the chart on page 60. You might also reproduce the chart on large chart paper.

4. After the students have listed as many repeated words and phrases as they can remember, reread the book and add more repeated words and phrases to the chart.

5. Discuss how this repetition makes the book more interesting and gives it a musical feel—much like the drum sounds "Tappidy-boom. Tappity-boom. Tappity-boom-boom-tap."

Traits Addressed

Word Choice, Voice, and Sentence Fluency

Repeated Word or Phrase

Example: "Mr. **Harry**-in-Charge" (Harry repeated)

Got Rhythm?

Titles for Teaching Sentence Fluency

In the Traits of Writing, **"Sentence Fluency"** is the melody and rhythm of carefully constructed language that is fluent, creative, and musical to the ear.

Evidence of Good Word Choice

- The writing presents clear images to the reader.
- The sentences are varied in length and style.
- The sentences are just as pleasant to the ears as they are to the eyes.

Books Used in this Chapter

An Angel for Solomon Singer by Cynthia Rylant. Orchard Books, 1992.

Dick and Jane: A Christmas Story by Larry Ruppert. Grosset and Dunlap, 2004.

Hello, Harvest Moon by Ralph Fletcher. Houghton Mifflin, 2003.

Heroes and She-roes: Poems of Amazing and Everyday Heroes by Patrick J. Lewis. Dial, 2005.

Library Lil by Suzanne Williams. Dial, 1997.

Night Noises by Mem Fox. Houghton Mifflin, 2003.

The Wheels on the School Bus by Mary-Alice Moore. HarperCollins, 2006.

Wonderful Words: Poems about Reading, Writing, Speaking, and Listening by Lee Bennett Hopkins. Simon & Schuster, 2004.

An Angel for Solomon Singer

by Cynthia Rylant; illustrated by Peter Catalanotto

Summary

Solomon Singer wanders the streets of New York City lonely and missing his Indiana home. He finds comfort and friendship in the Westway Café, a special place where dreams come true.

Prompts

Write a "Found Poem" using the words of this book.

Write about a place where you go to find comfort and friendship.

Lesson

1. Read *An Angel for Solomon Singer* aloud to students.

2. Explain that the class is going to choose one or two phrases from each page of the book that are either beautifully written, especially meaningful, or convey the intent of the page.

3. Read the book again, one page at a time, and let students choose a phrase from that page.

4. Write each phrase on the board or on chart paper in poetry format.

5. When you have completed the book, your class will have created a "Found Poem."

6. See the example of a "Found Poem" written by fourth grade students using *An Angel for Solomon Singer* on page 63.

Additional Activity

Allow students to work independently or in groups to choose a favorite picture book and create a "Found Poem" from it.

Traits Addressed

Sentence Fluency, Word Choice, Organization, Ideas, and Voice

An Angel for Solomon Singer

by Cynthia Rylant; illustrated by Peter Catalanotto

Found Poem

Written by fourth grade students at Richard Moore Elementary School in the Pasadena Independent School District.

K & S: Please fill in the blanks.

Hotel for men.

He didn't like it.

Oh what a difference a purple wall would have made.

Solomon Singer wandered

Wishing for the conversations of crickets.

He was lonely.

The Westway Café—where all your dreams come true.

He ordered tomato soup, a cup of coffee, and a balcony,

But he didn't say balcony out loud.

He came back the very next night.

The voices he passed sounded like the conversations of friendly crickets.

He felt at home.

The waiter's name was Angel.

Solomon Singer's dream had come true.

He doesn't feel lonely anymore.

Solomon Singer has found a place he loves.

Dick and Jane: A Christmas Story

by Larry Ruppert

Summary

Dick, Jane, and Sally play in the snow, bake cookies with Mother, and deliver cookies to the policeman, milkman, and postman saying "Happy Holidays!" to each of them.

Prompt

Write about something you do during Christmas/winter break.

Lesson

1. Read *Dick and Jane: A Christmas Story* aloud to students.

2. Using sentences and then paragraphs from *Dick and Jane: A Christmas Story* show and discuss with the students how to stretch sentences by adding or changing words to make the sentence more specific or interesting. A reproducible example is on page 65.

3. Put the students in groups of three or four. Give them a sheet of paper with an original sentence from *Dick and Jane: A Christmas Story* on it.

4. Have students number off in their group. Student #1 must add or change one thing in the sentence to make it more interesting, then pass it on to Student #2, etc. When the students are satisfied that they have an interesting sentence, they stop.

5. Have the students share the sentences/paragraphs with the class in order until they have re-written the entire book.

Traits Addressed

Sentence Fluency, Word Choice, and Organization

Sentence Stretching with Dick and Jane

"I am cold," said Sally."

Student #1: "I am **very** cold," said Sally."

Student #2: "I am **very** cold," **shivered** Sally."

Student #3: "I am **freezing**," **shivered** Sally."

Student #4: "I am **as cold as an ice cube**," **shivered** Sally."

Hello, Harvest Moon

by Ralph Fletcher

Summary

Ralph Fletcher's description of the Harvest Moon, and other things in nature, turns this book into a melody when read aloud.

Prompt

Write about your favorite piece of scenery.

Lesson

1. Read *Hello, Harvest Moon* to students.

2. Explain to students that imitation is the best form of flattery and discuss what that statement is really saying. Next, talk about imitating the writing style of good authors. Choose a couple of sentences for students to practice imitating, and write them on the board. Begin with an easy one and then advance to examples of personification such as example #2 on page 67. The third example invites creativity.

3. As students write their own compositions, they should incorporate some of their imitations.

Traits Addressed

Sentence Fluency, Ideas, and Word Choice

Examples of Imitation Sentences from *Hello, Harvest Moon*

Ex. 1: Page 10 of *Hello, Harvest Moon*

> *Birch trees shine as if they have been double-dipped in moonlight.*

Ex. 2: Page 21 of *Hello, Harvest Moon*

> *The harvest moon has its own work to do. It paints the wings of owls and nighthawks with a mixture of silver and shadow.*

Ex. 3: Page 7 of *Hello, Harvest Moon*

> *With silent slippers it climbs the night stairs, lifting free of the treetops to start working its magic, staining earth and sky with a ghostly glow.*

Heroes and She-roes
Poems of Amazing and Everyday Heroes

by J. Patrick Lewis

Summary

J. Patrick Lewis shares the stories of amazing and everyday people who gave of themselves to benefit others. The poetic and biographical information is a pleasure to read.

Prompt

Write about someone who is a hero or she-ro in your life.

Lesson

1. Read the first poem aloud to the students.

2. Write the last sentence on the board and have students compile a list of ways people can give:

   "To those simple people known by two simple words: *They gave.*"

3. Read aloud some of the titles such as "The Elementary School Teacher," "The Wonder Dog," "The Great One," and have students list some hero or she-ro categories of their own. Example: "The Leader," "The Fighter," or "The Strong One."

4. Next have them list the qualities of a person who might be put into each category that would make them a hero or she-ro.

5. Read several of the poems aloud to students, pointing out the smooth flow of the language and the variation of sentence beginnings.

6. Now have students write a poem about a hero or she-ro in their life. For extra credit, have students write biographical information about the person they chose.

7. As an extension activity, have students research famous people and compile a class Hero/She-ro book.

Traits Addressed

Sentence Fluency, Word Choice, and Organization

Library Lil

by Suzanne Williams

Summary

Lil had always loved books, so when she grew up to be a librarian, no one was surprised. Unfortunately, the town she lived in was full of television addicts. Lil's ultimate goal is get rid of the evil T.V. and turn everyone on to reading. She gets her chance when a big storm knocks out the power to the whole town. With the help of a local gang leader, Lil is able to get everyone reading.

Prompt

Write about a hobby or activity you enjoy and include at least one conversation in the composition.

Lesson

1. Read *Library Lil* aloud, asking students to listen to the fluency of the conversation between Bust-'em-up Bill and the Bartender.

2. Read just the conversation again, and ask students to list all the words used for "said" using the form on page 72 (yelled, roared, chuckled, laughed, spat, squeaked, growled, cringed, and grunted).

3. Discuss how the use of these words contributes to the fluency of the conversation and the tone of the scene. Also discuss the variation of the sentences and how they are constructed. Read the pages again just using "said" so they can hear how it changes the scene and makes it less exciting.

4. Discuss the overuse of the word "said" in writing.

5. Following the directions on page 73 for Linear Array in Writing, have the students make an array for "said."

SAID

negative ⟵――――――⟶ positive

6. Have students write a short paragraph using conversation imitating the one in the book. It can be real or imaginary. (A mini-lesson on dialogue punctuation might be needed here.)

7. Have each student read his/her conversation to the class and ask the audience to listen for other words for "said" to add to their list. Discuss the tone of each.

Traits Addressed

Sentence Fluency, Word Choice, and Conventions

Said

1.
2.
3.
4.
5.
6.
7.
8.
9.
10.
11.
12.
13.
14.
15.
16.
17.
18.
19.
20.

Linear Array in Writing

Students struggle with word choice in their writing. Word choice is one of the traits that will give them the depth and development needed to be successful on standardized tests and beyond.

SAID

negative ←—————————→ **positive**

Put an overused word up on the board and have students brainstorm a list of words that could be substituted for the listed word.

What other words mean the same as "said"? List the words, then place them on the line where they would fall between negative and positive connotations of "said."

Once you have exhausted the list, have students write a sentence replacing the word "said" with one of the words on the list and discuss how this changes the meaning of the sentence.

Example: John **said,** "I lost my lunch money."

John **cried,** "I lost my lunch money."

John **screamed,** "I lost my lunch money."

John **giggled,** "I lost my lunch money."

John **exclaimed,** "I lost my lunch money."

John **stated**, "I lost my lunch money."

Night Noises

by Mem Fox

Summary

Aging Lily Laceby sits in her cottage in the hills and drifts off to sleep. In her dreams, she hears many noises, which turn out to be family and friends coming to wish her a happy birthday.

Prompts

Write about a time when you were surprised.

Write about a special dream you had.

Lesson

1. Make a transparency of "A Passage from Night Noises" on page 75 which takes quotations from *Night Noises* and substitutes mundane words for the more interesting words that are in the book.

2. Discuss with students how the sentences on the transparency do not seem to flow smoothly.

3. Have students brainstorm words to replace the underlined words to make the story flow better.

4. Read *Night Noises* aloud to your students. Compare the words they have substituted for the underlined words with the actual words that Mem Fox used in the book.

5. Examine the way sentences in the book flow easily and inspire the reader to visualize the scene.

Traits Addressed

Sentence Fluency and Word Choice

A Passage from Night Noises

Directions: Replace the underlined words with more interesting words to make the sentences flow more smoothly.

One wild winter's evening, as Lily Laceby sat by her fire, snug and warm, she <u>went</u> off to sleep and began to dream. Butch Aggie <u>slept</u> at her feet. Outside clouds <u>went</u> along the sky, playing hide-and-seek with the moon. Wind and rain <u>fell</u> at the windows, and trees <u>hit</u> against the roof. Feet <u>went</u> up the garden path. Butch Aggie <u>raised</u> her head, but Lily Laceby went on dreaming. Voices <u>talked</u> in the bushes. Butch Aggie <u>moved</u>, but Lily Laceby went on dreaming. Eyes <u>looked</u> through keyholes. Butch Aggie's throat <u>made noise</u>, but Lily Laceby went on dreaming.

The Wheels on the School Bus

by Mary-Alice Moore; illustrated by Laura Huliska-Beith

Summary

The lyrics from the traditional song "The Wheels on the Bus" have been adapted to describe students and staff on their way to school on a big yellow school bus.

Prompt

Write about a trip on the school bus.

Lesson

1. If students are not already familiar with the traditional song, ask the music teacher to teach them "The Wheels on the Bus."

2. Brainstorm what words people from a school might say on the school bus as it drives along. Place their words on a transparency made from the "The Words on the School Bus" chart on page 78. Your students might want to add some school personnel who were not included in the book.

3. Read aloud *The Wheels on the School Bus* to your students.

4. Point out to students that sentence fluency is especially apparent when the words make up song lyrics.

5. When you are finished reading the book, you might want to have a sing-along and allow the students to sing this new version.

6. Notice that at least one person has been left out of the book—the principal. Have students create a

verse about the principal and any other people who might be missing from the book.

7. You might want to perform the song at your next school assembly.

Traits Addressed

Sentence Fluency, Voice, and Word Choice

The Words on the School Bus

Person from School	Words they might say on the school bus.
Kids	
Teachers	
Librarian	
Coach	
Nurse	
Lunch Servers	
Music Teacher	
Art Teacher	
Custodian	
Bus Driver	

Wonderful Words

Poems about Reading, Writing, Speaking, and Listening

by Lee Bennett Hopkins

Summary

Just listen to the beautiful melody of the language in this book. The selected poems are perfect to read aloud, as a choral reading, or as a paired reading. *Wonderful Words* begs to be heard.

Prompt

Write about something or someone that inspires you.

Lesson

1. Copy and cut apart the Poem Title Strips on page 80. Put the titles in a small flowerpot with the flower part showing. Have the students choose one.

2. Allow them a few minutes to study the poem and then have them give an interpreted oral reading for the class. Some poems may require pairs, and others even groups of four. You decide.

3. As each poem is read, have the students discuss what makes it good. Categorize the results. Was it word choice, sentence fluency, voice, ideas, organization, conventions, presentation, or a combination? Ask the students to cite examples.

4. Using some of the traits they have just discussed, have students write their composition about something or someone who inspires them.

Traits Addressed

Sentence Fluency, Word Choice, Voice, Ideas, Organization, and Presentation

Poem Title Strips

Metaphor

1212

Words Free as Confetti

How to Learn to Say a Long, Hard Word

Word Builder

I Am the Book

Share the Adventure

Let's Talk

Listen

Finding a Poem

The Dream

Writing Past Midnight

Night Dance

Primer Lesson

The Period

Let's Get Personal

Titles for Teaching Voice

In the Traits of Writing, **"Voice"** is the sense the reader gets that a real, honest, and personal individual is behind the writing and is speaking directly to them.

Evidence of Good Voice

- The reader feels a strong interaction with the writer.
- The piece of writing shines with personality.
- The piece of writing has a unique flavor and confidence appropriate for the purpose and audience.

Books Used in this Chapter

Dear Mrs. LaRue: Letters from Obedience School by Mark Teague. Scholastic, 2002.

Diary of a Worm by Doreen Cronin. HarperCollins, 2003.

I Wanna Iguana by Karen Kaufman Orloff. Scholastic, 2004.

The Mysteries of Harris Burdick by Chris Van Allsburg. Houghton Mifflin, 1984.

Rosy Cole's Memoir Explosion by Sheila Greenwald. Melanie Kroupa Books, 2006.

The True Story of the Three Little Pigs by Jon Scieszka. Penguin, 1989.

Voices in the Park by Anthony Browne. DK Publishing, 1998.

Who Is Melvin Bubble? by Nick Bruel. Roaring Brook Press, 2006.

Dear Mrs. LaRue: Letters from Obedience School

by Mark Teague

Summary

"Ike" LaRue is sent to obedience school to learn some "doggy manners." He voices his dismay through letters to his owner Mrs. LaRue.

Prompt

Write about a time when you were in trouble.

Lesson

1. Read *Dear Mrs. LaRue: Letters from Obedience School* to students, asking them to listen for phrases that reveal Ike's "voice." Make sure you show them the pictures of Ike's perspective and those of reality.

2. List some of the phrases on the board.

3. Have students write a letter from Ike to the Hibbin's cats or one from the cats to Ike. They could also write a letter about Ike's behavior from the teacher to Mrs. LaRue. Change Ike's character to FiFi— or even another animal—and write a letter to the owner.

4. Discuss what makes each change above have a different voice.

Traits Addressed

Voice and Organization

Diary of a Worm

by Doreen Cronin

Summary

Have you ever wondered what a diary written by a worm might say? Well, sit back and enjoy this insight into the life of an earthworm. Worm and his good friend Spider have adventures that are captured in diary form from March to August.

Prompt

Write a composition entitled, "Diary of a(n) _____."

Lesson

1. Discuss the kinds of things someone might write about in a diary. If a student already keeps a diary or journal, have them share the kinds of things they may write about. Guide them to say such things as feelings, emotions, events, celebrations, sad occasions, etc.

2. Read *Diary of a Worm* to the students. Point out the date at the top and the fact that sometimes days are skipped if nothing eventful happens.

3. Let the students brainstorm ideas for their composition:

   Diary of a Middle Child
   Diary of a Varsity Cheerleader
   Diary of a Basketball Player
   Diary of a Fifth Grader

4. Have the students decide on a time period and designate how many entries they must have.

5. In diary form, have the students put together their own "mini-book." Pictures and illustrations should be part of each page.

6. Have the students present their diary to the class.

Traits Addressed

Voice, Ideas, and Presentation

I Wanna Iguana

by Karen Kaufman Orloff

Summary

Young Alex is trying to convince his mother to let him have an iguana for a pet. This playful book goes back and forth in short notes between Alex and his mother as the negotiations go on. Alex uses all his persuasive charms to get what he wants.

Prompt

Write a letter to one of your parents convincing them to let you have something you really want.

Lesson

1. This book is wonderful for reader's theater. Have the girls take turns reading the notes from the mother and the boys take turns reading the notes from Alex.

2. Discuss how the notes are signed by the mother and Alex and some of the persuasive language that is used.

3. Discuss how the notes would be different if they were written from a girl (Alexa) to her father.

4. Have the students pair up and write their own notes with the boys asking for something and the girls answering by playing the role of mother, then switching roles and having the girls asking for something and the boys answering by playing the role of father.

5. Have the students do a reader's theater using their own works.

6. As an extension activity, have students do some research on the care and feeding of an iguana. A chart can be made comparing other animals by price, food, maintenance, etc.

Traits Addressed

Voice, Conventions, and Presentation

The Mysteries of Harris Burdick

by Chris Van Allsburg

Summary

The author presents a series of mysterious drawings, each with a title and caption. It is up to the reader to create a story using their imagination.

Prompt

Choose one illustration from *The Mysteries of Harris Burdick*. Using the title and the caption as a first line, write a story to go with the picture.

Lesson

1. Read aloud the introduction to *The Mysteries of Harris Burdick.*

2. Explain that the author, Chris Van Allsburg, wrote the introduction in first person so that his voice would be heard in the writing.

3. Show the class one illustration at a time, reading the title and caption provided by Van Allsburg.

4. Discuss whose voice each story would be written in.

   Example:
   Archie Smith, Boy Wonder—A tiny voice asked, "Is he the one?" This story should be written in the whispery voice of the dots of light.

5. Have each student choose a picture about which to write an original story.

6. Compile the stories into a class book.

Traits Addressed

Voice, Organization, and Presentation

Rosy Cole's Memoir Explosion

by Sheila Greenwald

Summary

Rosy's teacher gives the class an assignment to write about the most interesting person in their family. Rosy thinks she is the most interesting person and she knows the most about herself. Her sister tells her that she would be writing a memoir and that it would be a dynamite experience. After getting permission to write her memoir, Rosy begins writing and learns some important lessons along the way.

Prompt

Write about one important or exciting event in your life.

Lesson

1. Ask students if they have ever read the memoirs of a famous person. Be prepared to show some examples to students.

2. Make a list of what should be in a memoir.

3. Read Chapter 2, "Talent," and Chapter 3, "Romance," of Rosy Cole's Memoir Explosion to the students to show them how Rosy intends to proceed. This Web site is full of helpful resources for teaching memoir to students:
   www.emints.org/ethemes/resources/S00001109.shtml.

4. Have the students brainstorm some topics that might make an interesting story. Give them a copy of the "Who Am I Chart" on page 87 to get them thinking. Each story could become a chapter in their own memoir.

5. This could be a one-time assignment or something that is carried throughout the year. At the end of the year, students could compile their pieces into a scrapbook journal of their memoirs.

Traits Addressed

Voice, Organization, and Ideas

Who Am I?

Categories to begin thinking about the stories of my life:

People

Think about relatives, friends, teachers, community leaders ...

Places

Think about places I have lived, special places, vacations ...

Things to Do

Think about the things I like to do with friends, family, or alone ...

Emotions

Think about happy times, sad times, anxious times ...

Other

The True Story of the Three Little Pigs

by Jon Scieszka; illustrated by Lane Smith

Summary

The story of the *Three Little Pigs* is told from the point of view of the wolf. He claims he was really not a big bad wolf at all—he was framed.

Prompt

Rewrite a famous folktale or fairy tale from the point of view of one of the characters.

Lesson

1. Read or review the traditional story of *The Three Little Pigs*.

2. Read aloud *The True Story of the Three Little Pigs* to the class.

3. Explain that this version is being told from the point of view and in the voice of the wolf.

4. On the board, use a Venn Diagram to compare and contrast the two versions.

5. Instruct each student to choose a well-known folktale or fairy tale. Have them make a list of the characters and choose one who would have a different point of view about the story. This would often be the protagonist.

6. The students will then write the story again from that character's point of view, being careful to use the specific character's voice.

Traits Addressed

Voice and Organization

Voices in the Park

By Anthony Browne

Summary

This story is about different points of view on one event—a visit to the park. A young boy named Charles, his mother, a young girl named Smudge, and her father all tell of going to the park and how they perceive things to be.

Prompt

Write about a visit to the park told by three or four different points of view.

Lesson

1. *Voices in the Park* is wonderful for use as a reader's theater. Have four different students read the four voices. (Don't let them see the pictures yet.)

2. Using the chart on page 90, have students describe what each voice looks like, their age, etc. Discuss how a writer shows character traits through what a person does and says and what other characters say about them.

3. Now show the students the pictures in the book, and point out the font change, sentence structure, and punctuation of each new voice. Let them compare what they visualized with what is really in the book.

4. Have the students write a three- to four-part book using the different voices of the characters. They should incorporate some of the things they saw in the story.

5. Have the students do a reader's theater using their own works.

Traits Addressed

Voice, Conventions, and Presentation

Voices in the Park

by Anthony Browne

Voice 1	Voice 2	Voice 3	Voice 4

Listen for:

- How old do you think the person is?
- What does this person look like?
- What are some clue words that let you know what this person is like?

Who Is Melvin Bubble?

by Nick Bruel

Summary

Several people describe a young boy named Melvin Bubble. Each person has a unique perspective about who Melvin Bubble is because of the relationship they share with him.

Prompt

Write an autobiography of yourself from the point of view of five different people.

Lesson

1. Explain to students that this book is about an ordinary child, just like them. His name is Melvin Bubble.

2. Ask who they might ask if they wanted to know more about Melvin Bubble. Possible answers are his mom, dad, best friend, etc.

3. Read the story aloud, stopping to discuss how each individual person's description of Melvin Bubble sounds unique. Explain that each description is written using the individual voice of the person writing.

4. Have each student write a paper entitled, "Who Is (Student's Name)?" modeled after *Who Is Melvin Bubble?*

5. They should choose five different people to base the description of themselves on. They can either interview the people or use their own imagination of how that person would describe them.

6. After everyone has written their description, read the compositions aloud without revealing the students' names. See if the class can guess the main character of each paper.

Traits Addressed

Voice and Organization

Capitals, Periods, and Commas–Oh, My!

Titles for Teaching Conventions

In the Traits of Writing, **"Conventions"** means using capitalization, punctuation, spelling, grammar, usage, and paragraphing to make the piece of writing clear and understandable to the reader.

Evidence of Good Conventions:

- Punctuation guides the reader and contributes to clarity.

- There is consistent application of usage.

- There is mechanical correctness.

Books Used in this Chapter

Alfie the Apostrophe by Maria Rose Donohue. HarperCollins, 1949.

Brain Juice English: Fresh Squeezed! by Carol Diggory Shields. Handprint Books, 2004.

Eats, Shoots, and Leaves by Lynne Truss. Putnam, 2006.

The Hello, Goodbye Window by Norton Juster. Hyperion, 2005.

The Important Book by Margaret Wise Brown. HarperCollins, 1949.

Nouns and Verbs Have a Field Day by Robin Pulver. Holiday House, 2006.

Punctuation Takes a Vacation by Robin Pulver. Scholastic, 2003.

The Stinky Cheese Man and Other Fairly Stupid Tales by Jon Scieszka. Penguin, 1992.

Alfie the Apostrophe

by Maria Rose Donohue; illustrated by JoAnn Adinolfi

Summary

Alfie the apostrophe overcomes his fear of competing in the talent show with all the other punctuation marks and becomes the star of the show.

Prompt

Write about a type of competition. Examples: sports, talent show, spelling bee, dance, or music.

Lesson

1. Read the introductory page "About the Apostrophe" in *Alfie the Apostrophe*, and discuss with students the function of an apostrophe.

2. Read the remainder of the book aloud to students.

3. Copy and cut apart the cards on pages 95–96.

4. Have your students perform "magic" by choosing one of the cards and "magically" adding an apostrophe in the appropriate place to make a contraction or to show possession.

Trait Addressed

Conventions

let us	we are	should have
he will	we will	they will
did not	we would	you would
can not	was not	what is
are not	should not	were not

the children of the woman

the bone that belongs to the dog

the ticket that belongs to the man

the pet that belongs to the girl

the cookie that belongs to Maria

the home of the family

the boat that belongs to Kate

the lion that belongs to the zoo

the car that belongs to Don

the friend of the boy

Brain Juice English Fresh Squeezed!
40 Thirst-for-knowledge-quenching poems

by Carol Diggory Shields

Summary

This book is composed of 40 poems on the complexities and conventions of the English language.

Prompt

Write a poem about a punctuation mark of your choice.

Lesson

1. Choose any convention you are working on and read the poem about it from the book. You could spend an entire year highlighting one poem every week and doing activities with each.

   Examples:

   "Meet the Palindromes" pp. 36–37. Can you find them all?

   "Awesomely Alliterated" p. 38. Have students write some sentences with alliteration and vote on their favorite.

   "36 Ways to Say Cool" p. 45. Expand on this idea, seeing how many the students can come up with.

Traits Addressed

Conventions, Word Choice, and Presentation

Eats, Shoots & Leaves
Why, Commas Really DO Make a Difference!

by Lynne Truss

Summary

Each page spread shows how the position of a comma can change the meaning of a sentence.

Prompt

Write a composition about why it is important to follow the rules.

Lesson

1. Read *Eats, Shoots & Leaves* to the students.

2. Have students try their hand at making their own sentences in which moving a comma will change the sentence.

3. Have students draw pictures to show the different meanings.

Traits Addressed

Conventions and Presentation

The Hello, Goodbye Window

by Norton Juster; illustrated by Chris Raschka

Summary

A young child describes the special world of Nanna and Poppy's house as seen through their kitchen window, lovingly known as the Hello, Goodbye Window.

Prompt

Write about your special memories of being at the house of a grandparent or other relative or friend.

Lesson

1. Read aloud *The Hello, Goodbye Window* to students.

2. Point out that quotation marks are used only when the author writes down the exact words that people say. This is called a direct quotation.

   Example of a direct quotation:

   Poppy says, "What are you doing out there? You come right in and have your dinner."

3. Explain that a writer does not use quotation marks if the words are not the exact words of a character. This is called an indirect quotation.

   Example of an indirect quotation:

   Nanna says that she even used to give me a bath in the sink when I was little—really!

4. Explain that indirect quotations can be changed to direct quotations.

Example:

Nanna said, "I even used to give you a bath in the sink when you were little."

5. Duplicate and distribute the "Changing Indirect to Direct" worksheet on page 101 so students can practice changing indirect quotations into direct quotations.

Trait Addressed

Conventions

Name _____

Changing Indirect to Direct

Directions: Change these indirect quotations into direct quotations.

<u>Example:</u>

Indirect Quotation—Nanna says that she even used to give me a bath in the sink when I was little—really!

Direct Quotation—Nanna said, "I even used to give you a bath in the sink when you were little."

Indirect Quotation	Direct Quotation
Poppy says breakfast is his specialty.	
Nanna says it's a magic window.	
My teacher says that I am a good student.	
The coach said that the bat was broken.	
The server said that our food would be out soon.	
The forecaster said that the sun would shine today.	
The mail carrier said that I had received a greeting card.	

The Important Book

by Margaret Wise Brown

Summary

The Important Book is full of important things about a variety of objects, such as an apple, shoes, grass, and a spoon.

Prompt

Write about an object that is important to you.

Lesson

1. Read *The Important Book* to the students, pointing out the pattern used.

2. Duplicate and cut apart the cards with different punctuation marks on them. Make enough cards so that each student gets one.

3. Distribute the cards and—in small groups, pairs, or individually— have the students write the important thing about that piece of punctuation using the pattern set up in the book. See the pattern at the bottom of page 103 and the example on page 104.

4. Encourage students to share the various punctuation marks. Let them choose the important thing they like best for each punctuation mark to include in a book entitled: The Important Thing About Punctuation Is.

Traits Addressed

Conventions, Presentation, and Word Choice

Punctuation Cards

. **period**	**,** **comma**
? **question mark**	**!** **exclamation point**
" " **quotation marks**	**;** **semicolon**
: **colon**	**'** **apostrophe**

Pattern

The important thing about a _____is that _____. (defines the function)

What it is like: It's like a little shovel,

Where it goes: You hold it in your hand,

Where it goes: You can put it in your mouth,

Description: It isn't flat,

Description: It's hollow,

Statement: And it spoons things up.

Repeat the first line: The important thing about a _____is that _____. (defines the function)

The important thing about a period is that it lets you know when to take a breath when you read.

It's like a little stop sign,

You put it at the end of a sentence,

You put it where you want a complete idea to stop,

It isn't square,

It's round,

It brings everything to a halt for a moment.

But the important thing about a period is that it lets you know when to take a breath when you read.

Nouns and Verbs Have a Field Day

by Robin Pulver; illustrated by Lynn Rowe Reed

Summary

When the students in Mr. Wright's class leave the classroom for a field day, the nouns and verbs have a field day of their own and learn that they must play together in order to make sentences.

Prompt

Write about the nouns and verbs on a trip to the zoo. Use as many animal names as possible for the nouns.

Lesson

1. Read *Nouns and Verbs Have a Field Day* aloud to students once just for enjoyment.

2. Divide your students into the Noun Team and the Verb Team. Provide the Noun team with a stack of blue index cards on which to write down one noun per card as you reread the story. The Verb team should get a stack of yellow index cards to write down the verbs that they hear.

   The first person on each team gets the stack of cards. Once they have written a word, they pass the stack of cards on to the next person on the team, who writes the next noun or verb they hear. The students continue passing the stack of cards and writing nouns or verbs until you finish reading the book.

3. After you have finished reading the story, ask students to wander around the classroom with one of the index cards on which they have written nouns or verbs. The goal is to match up a noun and verb that will be the basis for a sentence.

4. After the students have found a partner, they should combine their noun and verb and add other words to make an elaborated sentence.

Traits Addressed

Conventions and Sentence Fluency

Punctuation Takes a Vacation

by Robin Pulver

Summary

One very hot day, Mr. Wright decides to give punctuation a vacation. As quotation marks and commas have fun in the sun, the class realizes that nothing makes sense without punctuation.

Prompt

Write about a time when you were on vacation.

Lesson

1. Read *Punctuation Takes a Vacation* to students.

2. Make the Punctuation Rules at the end of the book into a poster or transparency.

3. Have each student write a paragraph, of at least five lines, that includes four different punctuation marks. They will leave out the punctuation marks in their final draft, being careful not to leave spaces where punctuation would go.

4. Now have the students exchange paragraphs and find the "vacationing" punctuation in one another's work. Once they have found and placed all the correct punctuation in the paragraph, they will read the paragraph. For each returning punctuation mark, the student will read the rule for that mark.

Trait Addressed

Conventions

The Stinky Cheese Man and Other Fairly Stupid Tales

by Jon Scieszka and Lane Smith

Summary

Scieszka and Smith revise several well-known fairy tales such as Chicken Little (Chicken Licken), The Princess and the Pea (The Princess and the Bowling Ball), and Little Red Riding Hood (Little Red Running Shorts) with hilarious results.

Prompt

Write your own version of a popular fairy tale.

Lesson

1. Review the standard versions of the following folktales—"Chicken Little," "The Princess and the Pea," "The Ugly Duckling," "The Frog Prince," "Little Red Riding Hood," "Jack and the Beanstalk," "Cinderella," "Rumpelstiltskin," "The Tortoise and the Hare," and "The Boy Who Cried Wolf."

2. Read *The Stinky Cheese Man and Other Fairly Stupid Tales* aloud to students.

3. Explain that the creative use of format and font helps to make this book worthy of the Caldecott Honor for illustration.

4. Point out the following:

   a. Dedication Page—upside down

   b. Table of Contents—in the middle of the book, and the font is scattered

   c. The Really Ugly Duckling—the use of larger and larger font to emphasize the words

d. Blank page after Little Red Running Shorts (see text on previous page)

e. Jack's Bean Problem—creative use of size and shape of font

f. Giant Story—Collage of words and pictures

g. Jack's Story—the use of smaller and smaller font to emphasize the words

5. Allow students to search for additional creative formatting.

Traits Addressed

Conventions and Ideas

It's All About the Looks!

Titles for Teaching Presentation

In the Traits of Writing, **"Presentation"** is the visual invitation to the reader to enjoy a piece of writing.

Evidence of Good Presentation

- The piece of writing is appealing and pleasing to the eye.
- The piece of writing is legible and uniform.
- The piece of writing has a creative layout that "sells" itself to the reader.

Books Used in this Chapter

The Adventures of the Dish and the Spoon by Mini Grey. Knopf, 2006.

Can You See What I See? Once Upon a Time by Walter Wick. Scholastic, 2006.

Come to My Party and Other Shape Poems by Heidi Roemer. Henry Holt & Company, 2004.

Fairytale News by Colin and Jacqui Hawkins. Candlewick Press, 2004.

I Spy Christmas: A Book of Christmas Riddles by Jean Marzollo. Cartwheel, 1992.

The Jolly Postman and Other People's Letters by Janet and Alan Ahlberg. Little, Brown, and Company, 1986.

Look at My Book: How Kids Can Write and Illustrate Terrific Books by Loreen Leedy. Scholastic, 2004.

The Popcorn Book by Tomie de Paola. Holiday House, 1978.

The Adventures of the Dish and the Spoon

by Mini Grey

Summary

This is the continuation of the story of the cow jumping over the moon and the dish running away with the spoon. The dish and spoon go out into the world and fall into a life of crime before ultimately finding fortune and fame.

Prompt

Write about an adventure you have had.

Lesson

1. Read *The Adventures of the Dish and the Spoon.* Discuss some of the nursery rhymes students remember. You might want to also read several other nursery rhymes, since many students do not know them. The following Web site has hundreds set to music: www.smart-central.com.

2. Have students write their own adventure of any nursery rhyme character. (You might make a list of them to choose from: Jack and Jill, Humpty Dumpty, Georgie Porgie, etc.)

3. Have the students place their adventure on a large piece of construction paper. They should arrange the words and pictures in a creative way. The original verse must be somewhere on the page. See the example on page 113.

Traits Addressed

Presentation and Voice

Example of a nursery rhyme character's adventure

Jack and Jill
went up a hill
to fetch a pail of water.

Jack fell down
and broke his crown
and Jill came tumbling after.

After a long stay in the hospital,
the rest of the story goes ...

Can You See What I See?

Once Upon a Time

by Walter Wick

Summary

The author provides a search-and-find poem and picture for 11 classic fairy tales.

Prompt

Write a short poem which conveys the main idea of a classic fairy tale.

Lesson

1. Read *Can You See What I See?* aloud to the class, allowing students to search the pictures for the hidden items mentioned in the poems.

2. Have students select and read a classic fairy tale from the school library.

3. After reading their fairy tale, students should pick out 10–15 items that would be found in the tale.

   Example: The Three Little Pigs (straw, brick, sticks, wolf, tree, chimney, pig, barrel)

4. Students will draw a picture of the tale on the top half of the box on page 115, hiding the items they chose somewhere in the picture.

5. Students then use the bottom half of the box on page 115 to write a poem about their fairy tale picture using poems from *Can You See What I See?* as models.

6. Put the pictures and poems on a bulletin board for all to see and enjoy.

Traits Addressed

Presentation and Word Choice

Can you see what I see?

Directions: In the top half, draw a picture of the tale, hiding the items you choose somewhere in the picture. In the bottom half, include the items you chose in a poem. (The lines do not have to rhyme.)

Come to My Party and Other Shape Poems

by Heidi B. Roemer

Summary

This fun-filled, light-hearted book is full of concrete poems that take the shape of their subject.

Prompt

Write about something unusual or exciting that happened at a party.

Lesson

1. Read and share the poems in *Come to My Party*.

2. Have the students choose one thing that represents each season and write a shape poem about that subject.

3. Using the reproducible squares on page 117, put each seasonal concrete poem in a box.

4. Bulletin Board Idea: Cut the squares apart and make one big board using all of the cut squares from each student.

Traits Addressed

Presentation and Word Choice

Celebrate the Seasons

Fairytale News

by Colin and Jacqui Hawkins

Summary

When Mother Hubbard finds her cupboard bare, Jack runs out to find a job. He sees a sign reading PAPERBOY/GIRL WANTED. Jack applies for and gets the job of delivering the newspaper and they live happily ever after.

Prompt

Write about an event in your life as if it were written for your local newspaper.

Lesson

1. Read *Fairytale News* to the students.

2. Brainstorm some headlines for each fairy tale mentioned, as well as some others that the students know about.

3. Remind students that news articles include the 5Ws: Who? What? When? Where? Why? and sometimes How? Also remind them that the most important facts are in the very first paragraph with all the details following.

4. Have the students write a news article using one of the headlines they brainstormed earlier.

5. Put all the articles together for a class newspaper.

Traits Addressed

Presentation, Organization, and Word Choice

I Spy Christmas
A Book of Picture Riddles

by Jean Marzollo

Summary

Reading *I Spy Christmas: a Book of Picture Riddles* is like playing hide-and-seek with Christmas items. Each page contains a catchy rhyme which directs the reader to search for hidden holiday items in the illustration.

Prompt

Write an I Spy rhyme to correlate with a Christmas card illustration.

Lesson

1. Read *I Spy Christmas: a Book of Picture Riddles* aloud to students.

2. Discuss the way the author has used precise words as well as colorful adjectives to describe the hidden objects in each illustration.

3. Let each child choose a Christmas card from a collection that you have provided. (Collect old cards from friends and cut off the front cover for students to use.) An alternate source of cards is to have each child bring their own.

4. Have students write a verse that will identify five objects that the reader will find in the illustration on their card.

5. Glue the front of the card to an 8½ x 11" sheet of heavyweight paper. Have sudents cut out their rhymes and glue them below their pictures.

6. Compile all the students' pictures and rhymes into a class *I Spy Christmas* Book.

Traits Addressed

Presentation, Word Choice, and Conventions

The Jolly Postman and Other People's Letters

by Janet and Alan Ahlberg

Summary

The Jolly Postman rides his bicycle to deliver letters to fairy tale characters such as the Three Bears, the Wicked Witch, and Cinderella.

Prompt

Write a letter to one of the characters in a book you have read. Be sure the letter reflects facts from the book.

Lesson

1. Read *The Jolly Postman and Other People's Letters* aloud to students.

2. Show students the unique format that the correspondence takes. Some are letters while others are flyers, postcards, books, and birthday cards.

3. Provide each student with a 6 x 9" manila envelope, writing paper, and construction paper.

4. Each student will create some type of correspondence with a fairy tale character. The correspondence should address some aspect of the fairy tale.

5. Have students "mail" their letters in a class mailbox.

6. Letters can be shared with the class or posted on a bulletin board for all to enjoy.

Trait Addressed

Presentation

Look at My Book
How Kids Can Write & Illustrate Terrific Books

by Loreen Leedy

Summary

This book puts it all together. It is a step-by-step, student-friendly guide on how to write your own book. Don't let the delightful cartoon format fool you, this book is full of all the helpful information needed to get started on your own.

Prompt

Write your own book.

Lesson

1. Read the author's note addressed to young authors and artists in *Look at My Book* before sharing the book.

2. Follow the sequence put in place by the author, and let the writing begin.

3. As you cover each section, place the pertinent information on a poster for students to reference as they work.

   Example: Ideas—The words and art in a book start with ideas. Let the students come up with tips for getting ideas to add to the list in the book.

4. When the books are completed, have an author party for the students to share their works with each other as well as family and friends.

Traits Addressed

Ideas, Organization, Word Choice, Sentence Fluency, Voice, Conventions, and Presentation.

The Popcorn Book

by Tomie de Paola

Summary

Everything you ever wanted to know about popcorn is in this book. Its unconventional layout and humor make it a timeless favorite.

Prompt

Write about your favorite meal.

Lesson

1. Read and share *The Popcorn Book* with the students. Make sure they can see the unique layout.

2. Have students choose an object to research. They will take notes on as many facts as they can find. You may want to limit them to something edible like chocolate, apples, cookies, noodles, carrots, etc.

3. Show students many different layout ideas like brochures, comic books, advertisements, Web pages, annual report with graphs, menus, recipes, etc.

4. Have the students incorporate their data into a workable layout for their object.

5. Have each student present his/her project to the class.

Traits Addressed

Presentation, Word Choice, and Organization

Index by Author

A

Ahlberg, Janet and Alan. *The Jolly Postman and Other People's Letters*

B

Banks, Kate. *Max's Words*

Baylor, Byrd. *Everybody Needs a Rock*

Baylor, Byrd. *I'm In Charge of Celebrations*

Brown, Margaret Wise. *The Important Book*

Browne, Anthony. *Voices in the Park*

Bruel, Nick. *Bad Kitty*

_____*Who is Melvin Bubble?*

Byars, Betsy. *The SOS File*

C

Cates, Karin. *The Secret Remedy Book*

Child, Lauren. *Beware of the Storybook Wolves*

Chin-Lee, Cynthia. *Akira to Zolton: Twenty Six Men Who Changed the World*

Cronin, Doreen. *Diary of a Worm*

D

de Paola, Tomie. *The Popcorn Book*

Donohue, Maria Rose. *Alfie the Apostrophe*

E

Eschbacher, Roger. *Road Trip*

F

Fletcher, Ralph. *Hello, Harvest Moon*

Fox, Mem. *Night Noises*

G

Greenwald, Sheila. *Rosy Cole's Memoir Explosion*

Grey, Mini. *The Adventures of the Dish and the Spoon*

H

Hawkins, Colin and Jacqui. *Fairytale News*

Hest, Amy. *Mr. George Baker*

Hopkins, Lee Bennett. *Wonderful Words: Poems about Reading, Writing, Speaking, and Listening*

J

Juster, Norton. *The Hello, Goodbye Window*

K

Krauss, Ruth. *A Hole is to Dig*

L

Leedy, Loreen. *Look at My Book: How Kids Can Write and Illustrate Terrific Books*

Lewis, J. Patrick. *Heroes and She-roes Poems of Amazing and Everyday Heroes*

London, Jonathan. *Giving Thanks*

M

Marzollo, Jean. *I Spy Christmas: A Book of Christmas Riddles*

McKissack, Patricia C. *Goin' Someplace Special*

Moore, Mary-Alice. *The Wheels on the School Bus*

N

Numeroff, Laura. *If You Give a Pig a Party*

O

O'Connor, Jane. *Fancy Nancy*

Orloff, Karen Kaufman. *I Wanna Iguana*

P

Pinkney, Andrea Davis. *Duke Ellington*

Prelutsky, Jack. *Scranimals*

Pulver, Robin. *Author Day for Room 3T*

_____ *Nouns and Verbs Have a Field Day*

_____ *Punctuation Takes a Vacation*

R

Rayevsky, Kim and Robert. *Antonyms, Synonyms, and Homonyms*

Roemer, Heidi. *Come to My Party and Other Shape Poems*

Rosenthal, Amy. *One of Those Days*

Ruppert, Larry. *Dick and Jane—A Christmas Story*

Rylant, Cynthia. *An Angel for Solomon Singer*

S

Schotter, Roni. *The Boy Who Loved Words*

Scieszka, Jon. *The Stinky Cheese Man and Other Fairly Stupid Tales*

Scieszka, Jon. *The True Story of the Three Little Pigs*

Shields, Carol Diggory. *Brain Juice English: Fresh Squeezed! 40 thirst-for-knowledge-quenching poems*

Shulman, Mark. *Mom and Dad Are Palindromes*

Spinelli, Eileen. *The Perfect Thanksgiving*

T

Teague, Mark. *Dear Mrs. LaRue—Letters from Obedience School*

Truss, Lynne. *Eats, Shoots, & Leaves*

V

Van Allsburg, Chris. *The Mysteries of Harris Burdick*

W

Wick, Walter. *Can You See What I See? Once Upon a Time*

Williams, Suzanne. *Library Lil*

Z

Zweibel, Alan. *Our Tree Named Steve*

Index by Title

A

(The) Adventures of the Dish and the Spoon by Mini Grey

Akira to Zolton: Twenty Six Men Who Changed the World by Cynthia Chin-Lee

Alfie the Apostrophe by Rose Maria Donohue

(An) Angel for Solomon Singer by Cynthia Rylant

Antonyms, Synonyms, and Homonyms by Kim and Robert Rayevsky

Author Day for Room 3T by Robin Pulver

B

Bad Kitty by Nick Bruel

Beware of the Storybook Wolves by Lauren Child

(The) Boy Who Loved Words by Roni Schotter

Brain Juice English, Fresh Squeezed! 40 thirst-for-knowledge-quenching-poems by Carol Diggory Shields

C

Can You See What I See? Once Upon a Time by Walter Wick

Come to My Party and Other Shape Poems by Heidi Roemer

D

Dear Mrs. LaRue—Letters from Obedience School by Mark Teague

Diary of a Worm by Doreen Cronin

Dick and Jane—A Christmas Story by Larry Ruppert

Duke Ellington by Andrea Davis Pinkney

E

Eats, Shoots & Leaves by Lynne Truss

Everybody Needs a Rock by Byrd Baylor

F

Fairytale News by Colin and Jacqui Hawkins

Fancy Nancy by Jane O'Connor

G

Giving Thanks by Jonathan London

Goin' Someplace Special by Patricia C. McKissack

H

(The) Hello, Goodbye Window by Norton Juster

Hello, Harvest Moon by Ralph Fletcher

Heroes and She-roes Poems of Amazing and Everyday Heroes by J. Patrick Lewis

(A)Hole is to Dig by Ruth Krauss

I

If You Give a Pig a Party by Laura Numeroff

I'm In Charge of Celebrations by Byrd Baylor

(The) Important Book by Margaret Wise Brown

I Spy Christmas: A Book of Christmas Riddles by Jean Marzollo

I Wanna Iguana by Karen Kaufman Orloff

J

(The) Jolly Postman and Other People's Letters by Janet and Alan Ahlberg

L

Library Lil by Suzanne Williams

Look at My Book: How Kids Can Write and Illustrate Terrific Books by Loreen Leedy

M

Max's Words by Kate Banks

Mom and Dad Are Palindromes by Mark Shulman

Mr. George Baker by Amy Hest

(The) Mysteries of Harris Burdick by Chris Van Allsburg

N

Night Noises by Mem Fox

Nouns and Verbs Have a Field Day by Robin Pulver

O

One of Those Days by Amy Rosenthal

Our Tree Named Steve by Alan Zweibel

P

(The) Perfect Thanksgiving by Eileen Spinelli

(The) Popcorn Book by Tomie de Paola

Punctuation Takes a Vacation by Robin Pulver

R

Road Trip by Roger Eschbacher

Rosy Cole's Memoir Explosion by Sheila Greenwald

S

Scranimals by Jack Prelutsky

(The) Secret Remedy Book by Karin Cates

(The) SOS File by Betsy Byars

(The) Stinky Cheese Man and Other Fairly Stupid Tales by Jon Scieszka

T

(The) True Story of the Three Little Pigs by Jon Scieszka

V

Voices in the Park by Anthony Browne

W

(The) Wheels on the School Bus by Mary-Alice Moore

Who is Melvin Bubble? by Nick Bruel

Wonderful Words: Poems about Reading, Writing, Speaking, and Listening by Lee Bennett Hopkins